Unfolding Life

Understanding The Signs Of Life

by **Manoj Kumar Singh**

ISBN: 978-93-94749-08-5

Publisher

Power In Me Foundation

Book Name: Unfolding Life

Author: Manoj Kumar Singh

Format: Paperback

ISBN: 978-93-94749-08-5

Copyright

Publisher

Power In Me Foundation, H.No. 531, MIG-21, Near Subhadra Memorial Hospital, Opp. SBI Colony, Ganiyari Road, Waidhan, District- Singrauli, Madhya Pradesh-486886. Email id: mpowerinme@gmail.com, Mobile: 8851537816

Author

Manoj Kumar Singh, is Rex Karamveer Chakra, Bronze Medal recipient. Rex Medal is an international recognition by iCONGO recognised by the United Nations for People working in the field of Social Work and bringing a positive social change. He is a Visionary, Researcher, Life Coach and Trainer, Motivational Speaker, and an International Published Author. He firmly believes that words have the power to heal. Manoj has published 'Spices and Herbs' where he shares a guide for natural antibiotics and has also contributed towards scientific research. His fiction book 'The Last Act', 'Dil Ki Kalam Se', is his collection of poetry in the Hindi language. His other books focus on

'Networking for Jobs', 'How To Attain Inner Peace' and '55 Affirmations With Self Help Activities'.

Manoj expresses that poetry for him is a platform on which he communes with his divine soul. Poetry allows him to understand the deep desires he otherwise would neglect. His poetry is often soulful, spiritual, inspired by nature. When not writing he loves to pencil sketch, mobile photography or just meditate mindfulness. He shares his life learning as a life coach, helping people become internally strong and achieve inner peace.

He is a founder of a Trust, The Power In Me Foundation, where dedicated volunteers work for the welfare and education of people with rare diseases. He has profound clarity on his life purpose and is an advocate for Hemophilia and other rare diseases.

Preface

"You discover self only when you are ready to let go and believe in power of inner self."

This book 'Unfolding Life' is to get you in touch with your inner self. The inspiration comes from Mother Nature as it has many examples that help you to realise the truth of your life. Just like the biosphere in the Earth's realm, where life exists and all other realms merge together. Our life is a happy journey or a struggle, is defined by how we have understood the inner reality of life.

The following book is a simple spiritual journey where one starts to question about the existence of self, finding purpose of life and trying to understand the deeper connection with the universe. The nature as a teacher gives us signs, which when we are alert and understand them then life becomes easier. In this book the author has tried to understand the signs of life taking Nature as the reference point.

Acknowledgment

As years passed and I learned from my challenges, I could connect deeper to the nature and the universe.

I am grateful to nature and universe to constantly guide me towards better understanding of life.

I am thankful to the Divine for blessing my words while I was writing this book and I believe it will help other people to heal leading to a better life.

I am thankful to my parents, friends, teachers and students for all of them have contributed into my personal development and understanding of my life.

I am grateful to people who cheated or betrayed me for they taught me a lot and helped me become stronger.

Contents

Introduction

Is it imagination or the reality that scares you? For many it is the reality that troubles the mind. However, the mind has more power than what we have been taught to use. Most of the power is still hidden and you struggle to tap into it.

Then you will ask what is the way to bring it forth and use it? It is simple yet not that simple to understand. It is because to understand you first need to believe it and when you believe you will see the layers unfold to you one by one.

Mother nature is the best teacher you can ever have, if you really wish to learn about your life. Free your mind and give yourself to nature. This is a simple way to tapping into your true inner powers. In this book, mother nature is the source of unfolding life.

You want to get the best result from this book then just follow a simple meditation with breathing exercise. Sit in the padmasana pose with erect back bone no hunching. This posture allows flow of energy with maximum benefits. It also helps you to get better understanding.

Each chapter of this book are inspired by plants, animals, birds, insects and clouds etc. for they have some hidden messages from nature for understanding life. As you proceed each chapter will help to open your thought process to a higher level with greater understanding of life. And it will be your journey where you are unfolding life to get better understanding of life.

Chapter 1 "The Slow Growth"

Each one of us has wondered about the slow nature of growth that we have in life.

This growth is mainly realised at the financial levels as people tend to forget about the emotional and spiritual aspects of life. But the key here is that growth is always at the same rate it's the result of your efforts that start to show up as per your expectations.

No matter how strange or difficult things may look and feel in the start but when you are consistently growing the result is always fruitful. Mother nature is filled with many such examples where the first look may not be impressive but what comes after that is marvellous.

As beings we are part of mother nature and constant growth is inevitable. Plants have beautiful way of growth; it may be slow but is continuous. Even we can achieve it. All we need, is to realise our higher purpose and keep working towards it. Once we learn to do that, we can achieve anything in life.

The example of tree is exemplary because you can see that a small seed sown into the soil has only stored energy and some water around it to support its development. A human life is similar where you have to depend on your own inner potential to achieve what you desire in your life.

The growth may be slow in the beginning as you are less aware of your potential and your efforts towards your dreams give you the insight into your abilities. People who face failures and still have courage to go for their dreams are the ones who take the life lessons.

And with these life lessons they strengthen self to face the challenges without any difficulty. Here the rate of growth does not matter because then you are in sync with the continuous growth. This development or growth is associated with every aspect of your life covering emotions, spiritual and financial. Eventually, it has a more holistic effect on you as a being.

Chapter 2 "Life's Potential Is Beyond Time"

We are so trapped inside our own mind, overwhelmed by the expectations and pre-existing believes that we fail to see our own potential. A small dive into the nature lets us know that no matter, which time period you live in, your true potential can be only realised under right environmental conditions.

Our life is like the stacked buds with own time to grow and bloom. Look at plants even the same variety show different productivity even when given same environment. What is important that we accept the cumulative products and do not blame the one or two for less but try to find out why less. That's how we as humans should be doing, if less, then why and resolve it.

To make it clearer ponder on your life's situation where you have been blaming situations or people around you for the poor outcome. This could be you failing in your exam but you blamed on your parents for not getting you into a good tuition class. In their support maybe they could not effort to pay for it. There can be many more reasons but when you put yourself to finding those reasons, you may feel angry.

However, one of the reason's is that you did not focus well enough. Because if you would have then you could have at least got the passing marks. This holds true for any time period where parents may not be financially rich enough to be able to pay for extra expenses except the school fees. In this situation if the child considers his or her parent to be incompetent or non-supportive then that's a wrong thing to do. This negative thought over the period will accumulate and make the person more negative in life and unable to see the truth even when it is very clear.

Here one should be like a plant, happy in a small pot with good soil and enough manure with regular watering that produces flowers making people around happy. But when you put the same plant in a bigger pot with improved conditions, the blooms in it are bigger. Thus, it does not matter how much care or support you have but to know own potential which will help you bloom even under trying conditions and be happy. No matter which time period or time zone you live in, this simple realization will help you achieve your life's potential.

Chapter 3 "We Are Like Water To Each Other"

Water plays a very significant role in sustaining life. That even a small drop has energy and potential to give life. When you drink it, it cleanses you from inside while helping in other processes of the body too. And when you bathe it cleanses you from outside.

Similarly, our lives are twinned with people we meet. Some help us grow from inside while some other help us to grow from outside. You might have already heard that we meet people in our life who become part of the life or there are some meetings with people whom we meet for some time and separate.

For clarity, youth of today falls too often in love and gets their heart broken. They feel cheated and betrayed. Yes! This is a relationship lesson for them as they give trust to people without thinking much on it. And when the trust is broken, which they didn't expect leaves them hollow.

At times these negative feelings lead them to depression, trauma or anxiety like situations that have bad effect on their life. Also, there are people who cheat you in business or at work place. They teach you a lot in life that have deeper impact on you from inside. On the other hand, there are good people who love and care for you. They help you heal from inside and become strong. For outer development means your communication skills and your fashion sense etc. Friends help you evolve nudge you to go extra mile, here I mean by good friends not the ones who force you to drink or smoke. People who force you to take up bad habit can never be your well-wishers. Thus, you can see how people around you impact you and even you have an impact on them.

The water has powerful property to remove the toxins from inside the body, regulate the various processes within the body and cleanses you from dirt from outside. This protects you from developing any disease.

Reflect on it and see what role did you play in someone's life because in our lifetime we play both the roles.

Chapter 4 "At Times We Need A Little Bit Of Pruning"

Growth in life is possible when we continuously upgrade ourselves. Just few days back I picked some fresh lemons from our garden. It's wonderful to see that size has increased from previous lot. Yes, last batch was smaller in size and less attractive. All it needed was little pruning. It means cutting away some unwanted branches from top and side of a plant. This way we stimulate the plant to grow with little bit of manuring too. As it is in built for the plants to grow when cut.

Similarly, at times our life too needs pruning away of negative people, negative thoughts and negative situations because they are the ones which have held us back by not bearing fruits that we are really capable of.

The best you can do is to prune yourself and not depend on others to do it for you. I may seem difficult in the beginning because you have gotten used to the situation a bit and fear of change. Don't worry keep your hand on your heart and tell yourself about the positive things you wish for and take your pruning step. I hope your plant is pruned well enough from time to time to help you produce best lemons.

Chapter 5 "Talking To The Old Trees"

I love to take photographs of the nature around me, wherever I go. Sometime back I took photo of an old tree. It was dry with hardly any leaf or greenery on it. I found it majestic form of art from nature. I don't know why but I have always been attracted to old trees as if they want to share some stories with me or most importantly, they share learnings.

Similarly, we humans go through phases of childhood to youth to old age. In each phase we learn and grow. But in the end what remains is just the skeleton with thin skin covering it. And years of learning within only if there is someone ready to hear.

Look around you and talk to your elders. They have lot more to share than just old believes. Open your heart and mind as you are more flexible than them who are like this old tree. Left with only the wisdom of years of life learnings. At times these learnings may not be to your liking because present times are different but remember it is even more difficult for them as they have already got their roots deep. And your roots are still spreading in changing environment around you. One day you will be the old tree sharing your learnings.

Talking to the old trees help you know the mistakes that could be avoided, things that went wrong and things that will bring positive results.

Chapter 6 "Learning To Believe In Someone"

In life we are taught to believe in so many things that we have never seen yet we have to believe because someone we love believes in those things. People with rational minds tend to argue and question which is not wrong when it is about differentiating between right and wrong. Belief also has energy attached with it when you share it, you share that energy too. If the person, is you whom you shared your belief with then you become more energetic and work towards achieving it.

But this is only one person's belief working. What if there are more people believing in you the energy multiplies. This multiplied energy can now transform that person into a winner because now he will not be afraid. Appreciation and words of encouragement are ways you show your belief in that person that has power to yield amazing results.

Try appreciating a person who is trying and see the results change. You will also see that then the hard work transforms into a smile on the face of that person. Even the stress is gone. It is the power you share with your belief in them.

I believe when you believe in self, it's half the battle won but when you believe in someone, you help create a winner.

Chapter 7 "Being Rich Resides In The Attitude You Posses"

Some of the richest people have empty pockets, wounded souls, plenty of determination and never say die attitude.

We as society have been groomed to believe that rich people are those who live a lavish life. They have all they want because their bank balance is beyond imagination. And that prompts others to be like them.

However, the truth is that majority of these lavished life dwellers have poorest of hearts. Whereas people who have less of money lavish have richest heart because they have learned to appreciate what life has to offer. That doesn't mean they are not ambitious rather they have learned to enjoy the process and celebrate achievements by others too. They never give up on their dreams and on people they believe in. They are determined souls having faced various life challenges and yet never give up.

It is never about how swelled your bank account is, rather it's about how healthy it is. A healthy bank account means you have appropriate amount of money that you can use to fulfil your desires and wishes of your loved ones. Also, it is sufficient to keep you afloat during an emergency. You are left with a happy heart, home and life. I think that is what most of us want from our life, that makes us rich.

Chapter 8 "What Are You Holding On"

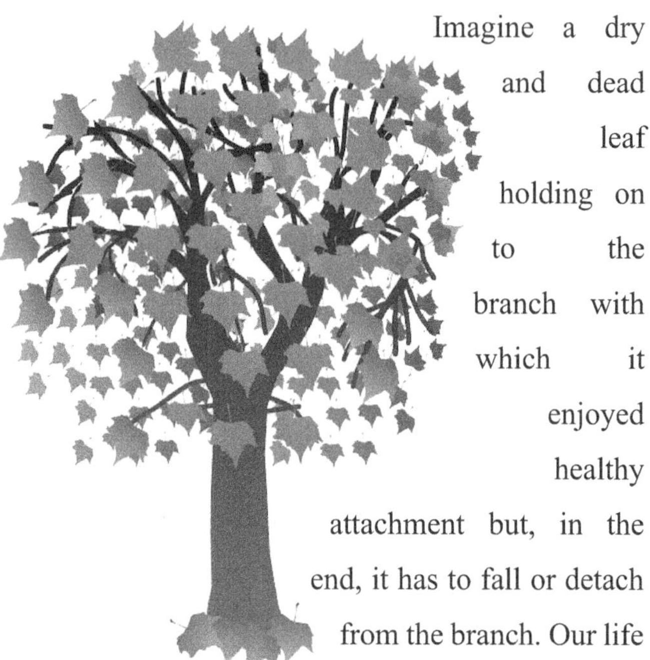

Imagine a dry and dead leaf holding on to the branch with which it enjoyed healthy attachment but, in the end, it has to fall or detach from the branch. Our life is also like that leaf and branch with which we are holding on to are what we have been taught.

When we start and life takes its full glory it teaches us many things. It is there when we must learn to detach from something and make way for new thinking. But majority of us do not like to detach from that branch because we were supposed to enjoy and be happy with it. And this continues even unto death. However, death is the biggest reality of life as one who is born has to die one day. So, we must me mindful of what we wish to hold on to when we take that last breath.

For me biggest satisfaction is of how many lives I could touch and help bring a positive change for them. What I am holding on to is peace for all and no grudges against anyone. Be mindful of your thoughts which are somehow leading you to attachment to things that are becoming self-sabotaging.

Chapter 9 "Challenges Are For Learning And Growth"

Put your imagination to some work and imagine how our life is lot like a branch of a tree. It can grow straight, be strong and produce flowers with fruits. If a storm breaks the branches, the tree heals to produce new branches. These challenges faced by the branches of the tree are the obstruction in growing path because learning is needed.

The learnings are to help us to sprout again as life is to move forward with new hope making the path meant to new beginning. The broken branch learned the lesson and waited for the right time with hope to regrow. It is observed that the point of regrowth is healthy. You will find the leaves greener and the sight will give you a sense of hope.

The way you look at the challenges will determine whether you will learn and grow working though it or you will end up struggling. Let us grow into our best self while we live towards our dreams through layer by layer of unfolding life.

Chapter 10 "Be Scared Still Love"

One of the most difficult things in life is to love and to reciprocate love without fearing, doubting or being scared. At times with so much negativity around we tend to fear a lot. And in this fear, we lose our true selves. This lost self, fears even the good that may happen to it. It loses the smile that makes it awesome.

That true self is one which loves self and everyone. It trusts self through gut feelings and others as bonds with them. However, as, more of the world and life happens we lose it all. We are trapped into the self-doubt, which never lets us out grow it.

But best is when we let ourselves heal while we learn to trust again. This trust can be found with knowing that it is ok to be scared. Knowing failure is not end but a learning for new beginning. This way you will start loving self again that is a step towards able to open the heart to love people around. It will help share love with others.

I have decided that I may be scared but I still choose to love. After reading this what did you decide? Do let me know!

Chapter 11 "Your Happiness Determines Your Fragrance"

Ever wondered why two same flowers grown near to each other but slightly different microenvironment has different sizes. But emit same fragrance and are equally beautiful when blossom?

The simple reason is that they are happy even when the law of competition is working for getting the nutrition from soil and space around.

Why are they happy? Because they don't compare with what other is getting but are focused on self to become better version of oneself under whatever circumstances they are put to grow (Read these lines again).

And they fight the challenges they face without comparing. This we humans have forgotten. For example, even some fond memories of growing up bringing cheer are turned into agony by comparing it with someone else's journey during the same period. That they had better life.

One thing that goes missing is you don't realise the starting point. Where you started and with what in hand.

Also, same applies for every other human around you. Each one is busy destroying the happiness by a mere comparison with someone else who has their own life journey. So, the next time your mind starts to wander become the flower that knows how to be beautiful and smell lovely. You know why? It is because the world needs to know the true you and feel the beauty you hold within yourself.

Chapter 12 "It Is Your Adaptability That Determines Your Sustainability"

When we talk about a plant or a tree, mostly we talk about how majestic the tree looks or about its flowers and about the fruits. Again, if it is hardwood then we talk about its usage into making homes or furniture. The leaves are often most under spoken about. But these leaves carryout photosynthesis and help into making food for the plant and us.

However, similar to the flowers they too have adapted through their evolution into different forms to supply food for plants and oxygen for us. They take enough sunlight and carbon dioxide that's necessary and give out oxygen and water vapour at different time at varied rate of process.

Also, some adaptations are that help to minimum loss of water and protection from the prospective predators. They teach us importance of keeping control and adapting as per the environment for better sustainability without harming the surroundings.

In fact, they make surroundings better place for other creatures to inhabit. The nature is filled with many more examples of adaptations by different organisms that blend with the nature for proper sustainability of the organism. We humans have lost the bear thing that makes us home that is to adapt keeping others around us in mind too. Such that they do not get harmed. This us the greatest need for us humans to learn in present time.

Chapter 13 "Let The Layers Of Life Open To Grow"

Let us go into the nature again and see what does  growth mean and how it happens? In plants the layers open one by one into the leaves and marking the growth. The growth that is signified by formation of stronger stem and branches lead by the leaves in the apex.

Our lives are also similar to how plants grow. We grow through the unfolding of the layers of life, which bring life learning. These learning are important for making us stronger just like the stem of the plant, that determines how it faces challenges thrown in by the nature.

The shades of leaf whether dark or light or patchy are results of the external environment and internal balance. The external environment being availability of proper sunlight, water, nutrition, protection from predators and any extreme climatic or natural condition that may limit the overall growth of a potentially large plant.

As we grow our personality and overall being are the shades of experiences we had in our life. Whether it is good or bad, all accumulate into memories. After this growth is our choice that comes from constant struggle to give in to the temptations or hardships. By giving in we choose mediocrity and by choosing to be comfortable with the unfolding of the life, we choose growth. It also makes us strong to face any challenge that may come along in this journey called life.

Chapter 14 "Holding On To The Hope"

There is a beautiful flower in our small home garden. It blooms on a thorny plant that most part of the year is thorns and few leaves. This plant is a succulent species of plants. It requires less of water and does not even get bothered if you do not take care of it. Like you forget to water it on time or even days, it would still be happy and green. Probably it believes in hope and that keeps it growing. This eventually gives flowers with bloom beautiful enough to make you happy with its sight.

Life is similar to this succulent filled with challenges. And most of the time not believing but giving up the hope for goodness in tomorrow. But when the fruits of the hardship come, they bring with them the beautiful feeling of satisfaction. Until then the time is filled with mixed emotions, mostly frustrations and little bit of hope.

When you decide to cling on to that little hope you make your way to that moment of happiness and satisfaction. A heart filled with satisfaction feels less of negativity and can muster courage to keep going amidst the tough time.

I have always hold on to hope. What are you holding on to?

Chapter 15 "It Is About True Unfolding Of Life"

I have constantly spoken about life being in layers which, we need to discover during our stay on earth. In these layers of life, which one is on the top varies from person to person. As each one of us have a different environment for growth and so varies our response to that environment.

Those layers are just like the beautiful layers of the flowers with their florets unfolding to give it, it's beauty. The true beauty of the flower comes with the balanced opening of all the layers together making it look full. But when any layer is different and takes time to unfold, it gives a different look to it than usual. However, one thing that always remains with the flower is its essence of inner fragrance and a sweet nectar that feeds the honey bee.

The human life is also like that, even if we have something that's not complete or missing still, we have that innate essence of love and kindness that spreads across to unfold into a beautiful life. All we need to do is to recognize the hidden layer that becomes less visible due to dirt and dust of worldly demands.

The true unfolding happens when we recognize that something still needs to be discovered and start working towards it. In this path we help others too in finding their peace.

Chapter 16 "Life Goes On"

The birth and death are two ends of life. And we live our life in between the both. The emotions, the feelings and the ups and downs are all what makes up your life. You meet people who stick with you for life and you have people who teach you lessons for life.

There are people you love but never have with you and there are people you spend your life with. There are days when you are happy and then there are days when you are sad. There are times when you feel lonely and there are times when being alone is solitude.

The sickness or the state of wellbeing bring their learnings. Fear of dying when you know it is the only truth of life. That the one who has taken birth will one day leave this world. When you gain true insight about life, you understand challenges help make you strong. The lesson to learn is that life goes on. Keep your faith in the process and keep moving.

Chapter 17 "Nature The Guru"

Isn't it wonderful when you have sown a seed in your pot, garden or your field and when after some nurturing you see those seeds turn into the little plants?

These plants then bloom with beautiful flowers. The flowers spread happiness and hope to lives near it. Isn't your life one seed with immense potential? And under right nourishing environment you realise your potential.

Mother Nature has many life lessons to teach us, only if we keep our eyes open. Flowers have deeper impact in our lives with their colors, fragrance, pattern, time of blooming and how they sustain under pressure.

Nature is an ultimate teacher guiding us at every step, sending us signs what is the right path to follow. And you know what the path that gives you good night sleep, a smile when you are down and a hope for better future, that my dear friend is the path to follow.

So, whenever possible you go and meet the guru called Nature. She will always embrace you with wisdom for your harmonious life. In turn never forget to show your gratitude towards nature by planting more trees and preserving the lives of flora and fauna.

Chapter 18 "Respect The Changes"

A typical human life is always a search. This search is never ending as we seek stability in life. Because the so-called stability is linked to your status in society and your responsibility towards your family. It is said that a person who has good job meaning has source of income is stable and happy. If the person has property, then he or she is stable. They are perfect for having a family and happy life. But the life is more than this fairy tale belief.

And the time never remains the same. One day you are happy other day you may be unhappy because something happened that was not good. It is similar to the clouds in the sky which change their patterns regularly. Our life is also the same, it keeps changing.

You can try to find the similarities but each pattern or time is different from the other. These differences or changes are very subtle that may not be visible to naked eye or we can say to the mind that is trapped in the diversions of life.

We tend to suffer because of these changes if they are not as per our thinking. We try to manipulate things to ensure it is our wish that is achieved. But forget about the other people too and their happiness. However, when we learn to respect the changes, we learn to have a better life that is more fulfilling. Accept the life as it unfolds. This may sound difficult and remember it is tough but very satisfying once you have learned to master it.

Chapter 19 "Connecting With Nature"

It is a known fact that each human is born with an

innate tendency to be close to the nature. However, the corrupt demands of the world, ego and his hunger for power and money takes him away from nature. If you are not spending enough time in nature, you will lose your good mental health state and face many more problems that remain invisible until after years of accumulation they finally show up.

For a life to survive and blossom, it needs love and nurturing. That is the very thing mother nature takes care of. Rain is her love and care for all to ensure that life sustains and the cycle of life continues. When you look deep enough, you will see that it is the life energy that is shared with everyone.

And many times, it is a therapy of nature in the form of calmness and peace felt deep in the heart without you thinking too much. World's simplest doctors give simple treatments with greater effects. Nature is a powerful healer creating simple yet highly effective therapies.

When you spend some time in nature you get to feel them. And when you connect to avail them, the only fees that that you pay back to mother nature is living happy and healthy life.

Chapter 20 "Finding The Reason For Your Light"

It is ok to be thoughtful of what you need to do in life and how to go about it. But putting yourself or people around you into the stress will not bring the true results. And you may struggle that may put you into a darkness where you are unable to think properly.

To simplify, the darkest days of life are the indications of the hidden light within you. Just like a seed that has life within. It waits in the dark buried inside the soil for this time to pass. It too has an uncertain future but somehow it knows the reason for its light/ existence.

This is how life works, sometimes you have to slow down or may be take a pause just a little while. Hold your breath, reclaim your strength and rise again to the tiny plantlet with the potential to be the giant plant it is meant to be.

Before you get swept away with the notion of giant tree, remember not every seed is tree. It can be the flower, cereals that feed, small shrubs with berries or medicine plant that heals people. You don't have to worry about how tall you get but let the potential find its way. All you will need is to just nurture with love and care. Then you will feel and see the magic.

Chapter 21 "The Realm Of Life"

Our life is simple yet complicated with multiple layers to it. These different layers of life are like different realms of nature. These realms comprise of water, air and land. They are all important and supporting to each other. Life is only possible when all these realms work together. This life sustaining realm is called biosphere.

Similarly, key to a wonderful life is, accepting different layers of emotions and relations in it. It is when you realize this aspect and work in alignment with it you experience abundance. Meditation is a great way to build that power within you. It helps you to get in touch with those realms/layers of life that somewhere you have lost touch with.

Your healthy life is determined by the healthy realms that make it up. When you are mindful and work towards slowly igniting each realm to reach their maximum potential giving you the best life.

Chapter 22 "Each Life Is Connected"

The very first step that you need to take when searching for life is to know the true meaning and see the deeper connection between the universe around. Nature has diverse life forms. And she has all the resources to take care of every life just like a mother takes care of all its children.

The nature works very deeply with the connection among these life forms. Be it the microorganisms who are invisible to naked eyes to the largest organism blue whale, that cannot be kept hidden. When you open your heart and let the vibes of universal energy flow in, you will see that deeper connection with all.

Then you will start to respect each life form and the unseen connection between every form of life. When this happens, every life prospers. It is time to slowly bloom with balance and help in restoring of nature.

Chapter 23 "Perseverance And Patience"

Humans over the time have unlearned the art of being patience. Whereas, the nature teaches us the lesson to have patience. Nothing in nature happens overnight. In fact, everything is the cumulative effect of regular changes that are happening. Even the seasons happen at their fix time which governs how life forms evolve and sustain.

True growth is achieved only when we combine patience with constant efforts. These efforts or your perseverance to keep on working for your growth starts to show brilliant results in due course of time. And there comes one day when you bloom. At this stage you reach the state where you want to pass that true growth to others. Here you find the purpose of life is to learn and share.

Yes! These learnings from your life journey when shared help other people to cope better with their challenges and be strong even in difficult times. All you need to do is to keep your patience intact while you persevere.

Chapter 24 "Your Growth Is Someone's Hope"

Have you seen a bird flying high in the sky and dreamt if you could fly, then what you would have done? Similarly, our achievements or growth are like flying in the sky or you can say we attain a height in our flight of life. However, this height is not only for us but it's for some other people too.

These people are ones who have lost hope or believe that happiness is no more their right. They compromise their lives and dignity. But when come from them, whether a man or a woman or someone from a special community or with any disability. You become their hope with which they can find confidence. This confidence gives them the courage to flap their wings and dare to fly.

This small hope gives them the power to bring a change. A change that's not only for self but an overall transformation of the world. So, if you are tired, then take some rest but do not stop as your efforts bring the change. The change that gives courage to those fearful hearts and strength to their wings of desire to rise. You are someone's hope for better tomorrow. Keep going keeping this simple thing in mind.

Chapter 25 "Live Every Moment"

We as a human have been gifted with the mind. A mind that has power to take rational decisions based on the evaluation of experiences we go through. However, it is also the main cause of our sufferings. We do not put it into proper use rather fill it with insecurities, fear and ego. Failure to entertain them leads to dissatisfaction, which builds to suffering.

When you learn to better understand self and emotions, you get a better life. We plan and try to live a long life but fail to really live the life. Here maturity is not about how many years you have lived but how many moments you have experienced.

Because these experiences ultimately define your life's outcome.

It is this important skill of living every moment that determines peace of mind and self-growth. You are able to get the best out of those moments. You enjoy sharing love and caring with people around you. This simple understanding of life helps in blooming of the life that is not only for self but for the community.

Chapter 26 "Embrace The Failure"

Failure is an in inevitable result when you dare to dare and chase your dreams. It is connected with the feelings of being dejected, rejected and moments of grave uncertainty. You would be called for things that you could not achieve because you told so. And these will be the people who say they are there for you but would not support you. Anxiety and fear surround you as the path is unclear.

Do not worry about what others are saying because if someone has not helped you in your difficult time, their opinion should be taken with discretion. The best option is a mindful look at all the things and letting the feelings flow with intention set at right.

You will find the path no matter how dark the night. Just a simple practice will help you learn from the life lessons called failure by some. The life will find its purpose and the drive will then never end leading to all you ever dreamt of. In simple words when you learn to embrace your failures in the path filled with greater efforts towards your dreams will make you strong with more experience.

Chapter 27 "It Is All About Unconditional Love"

Unconditional Love is simple yet more powerful form of love. Yes, love has types too as different people define it in their own ways. However, love that expects nothing in return is more powerful as it means you are just loving that person but it doesn't mean you will allow abuse or exploitation.

Many people think love is to even bare bad things. Wait a minute, it's wrong that way you make that person even more abusive and disrespectful. Unconditional love means you did not sacrifice your dignity even if the person you love doesn't understand that. You can still continue to have a peaceful life with love in your heart.

When you put your loving heart out there in search of love with detachment to the expectations. You make those powerful changes within yourself that help you stay strong and not be desperate for love. This situation is powerful for both in love as they share the vibes connecting their hearts and care for wellbeing of each other.

Chapter 28 "Recognize Your Own Pace To Growth"

Did you ever take some time out for yourself to relax and think on the life you have had? I believe majority of you reading this have said no or would be saying not often. Well! that is truth and we are all similar in that way. We forget to think about the most important person, which is we ourselves. In the world where you are taught to keep on competing without taking a break, you believe fast is the way to go.

But in reality, it takes a lot of patience and growth to bloom into a beautiful flower. Aren't we a flower spreading our fragrance into this world? Starting from a mere floral bud, there are many stages of growth. Similarly, every individual has its own pace of growth into what they are to become. Some achieve it early others take just a little bit more time. Keep patience, keep working and never give up.

Because when you recognize your pace then you will feel the contentment in the heart without any mental pressure. It is then you are aware of your true potentials and with progressive mindset you will focus on improving your skillsets than wondering about the non-existing competition.

Chapter 29 "Rain Drops And Life"

Raindrops and life are bit similar. You know why? Because when it drizzles, it is so easy and fun. But when overwhelms both pour without being distinguished from each moment. It settles on the leaf of hope and faith. Then sparkles like a pearl.

I became bit poetic but isn't it the reality of life that when things are going well, you feel happy, smooth and relaxed. It is like the tiny rain drops as drizzle float in the air gives you happiness. However, when things are difficult in life you cannot control your emotions and tears trickle down from your eyes. You are not able to stop yourself. It is similar to large drops of rain that pour down heavily damaging things when they fall.

We should be the rain drops that bring balance in nature leading to greenery everywhere. Our life should be like the rain that fills the dry water bodies to help other lives. We should help the dry land by ending its thirst and preparing it for new cycle of life. What are your raindrops saying today?

Chapter 30 "Transition To Growth"

Transition! Well, it is not an easy process, especially when you are born in a family where middle-class mentality *i.e.*, Thinking only within the box is deeply rooted. Under this situation your dreams become uncomfortable for people around you who should be your support system.

This is the first block to your growth. They have seen limited money and limited everything. So are scared to take that extra step, sometimes called as risky factor. No matter how hard you try you have been pulled back, because you are attached and the same limited energy surrounds the whole family and its members.

There are sudden losses due to health, vehicle, debt or any other. This demands detachment to save self from frustration and regular blocks. Detachment from results and disclosing your projects to people with limiting mindset because they infuse fear that brings hindrance.

The way forward is to up your efforts, plan well and take support of right people who believe in you and your vision. Once you are able to break this, you will pave the way for entire family to abundance and growth.

This is that crucial transition that you need to make either alone or with the family, if they wish to. All you need to do is keep working through these limiting waters to the destination that is worth making efforts.

Chapter 31 "All It Takes Is A Step"

Good times or bad times, our deeds determine how long these periods exist in our life. When things are unwell and everything around us seems unfavorable, we are trapped. The question is, are we? Well life at various moments has taught me that these circumstances remain until we decide and take that first step to resolve it.

This applies to every aspect of life including the relationships, work, health or any other thing. It does not matter whether the step taken is very small because till it aims at positive outcome it will impact your life. Always remember small steps together lead to bigger results. Trust self and put genuine efforts in form of small steps no one can stop your growth.

It feels a bit scary in the beginning but when you have decided to move with clarity in the head you will slowly feel the fear go away. I have taken my step, have you taken your yet? Lots of love and blessings to all who have dared to take that step.

Chapter 32 "The Chase For Perfection"

Few years back if you talked to me, I would be Mr. Perfectionist wanting everything perfect. In fact, I would get irritated if things were not done properly and organized manner. But the life taught me an important lesson that nothing is perfect.

When I look at life and world around me then I see that there are many old me in the society. They are daily chasing perfection and getting frustrated. The energy that flows through us is also ever changing so no perfect form is retained. You may have an illusion of seeing something as perfect but in reality, it is not.

The thing to remember is that it's the work that is achieved in the end that matters. Today, I have learned to love my imperfections. Because that gives me leverage to improve and better myself each day. With this I move closer to my life's purpose.

If you want to really understand your life then think on what you are chasing? The answer to this simple question will give you more clarity in thoughts. And clear thoughts bring better results in life with every effort you take.

Chapter 33 "Life Blooms In Stages"

Are you ready to put your thoughts into the right realm? If your answer is yes then the following lines are easy for you. Otherwise just bear with me. Ever noticed different stages of blooming of a flower right from the stage of bud to complete blooming into a beautiful flower. This flower is enchanting with color and fragrance.

Our life is also a flower in the process of blooming. The stage of bud is when you are going thing learnings of life. The challenges you face are just like the environment and manure for the process of blooming of life.

The achievements in your life indicate you are blooming just the right way you are supposed to and your true beauty is revealed to the world. When you understand that you have to go through these stages of life to bloom, you will learn to enjoy every unfolding the life has to offer to you.

Chapter 34 "Happiness Should Come With No Reason"

When we learn to be happy for no reason, we learn the true art of living. Because then we learn to truly appreciate the life itself as being alive in itself is a great reason to be happy. Your happiness is a form of gratitude and prayer to the divine that you trust the process and believe in goodness present in the universe.

Also, when you are happy you spread that happiness to people around you. The positive vibes that you share may help someone fight the challenges they may have in their lives. Again, being happy helps even you take right decisions that are not always influenced by the circumstances.

Try and fill your heart with sense of gratitude. You will feel the peace within and the happiness that originates from non-attachment to circumstances or results. It is for this reason I chose to spread love and happiness. What about you?

Chapter 35 "Life Is A Reflection"

It was a sunset when we were returning from our village and there was reflection of the Sun and a tree on the car roof. The reflection was so real yet it was only the reflection of the truth. Similarly, our lives are also a reflection of what we dream and what we work for.

The desires that we may have always shape up the reality of the reflection called life. The smile may be the reflection of abundance but it can also be a reflection of resurrection, a hard-fought battle.

Have you ever given it a thought about the person who stands in front of you and the wounds that may be hidden behind the reflection? The reflection he or she portrays in front of you. You can see the reality and feel the true connection.

With this you will be also able to reflect your brilliance to the world. And when these different reflections come together, they sow the seed of a beautiful world, where each life is a happy reflection.

Chapter 36 "Uncertainties Are Nudges Towards Your Dream"

Are you the one, who gets anxious easily? Or you are the one who dares to take bold steps in life? While you are thinking on the answer let us ponder on the path we follow towards our dreams. It is up to you to follow the path of life towards the journey of your dreams.

This path may not always be what you imagined or remains the same when you started but the importance is in your journey that you continued to follow. When you learn to embrace the uncertainties that may come along in your journey towards your dreams, your life becomes lot peaceful and hurdles become challenges that are easily overcome.

It is this ability that you gain the strengthening through challenges of life you start making headways towards your dreams. The steps are with lot more confidence which yield you positive results. Get ready and enjoy these uncertainties as the nudges towards your dreams.

Chapter 37 "The Pains You Endure Make You Strong"

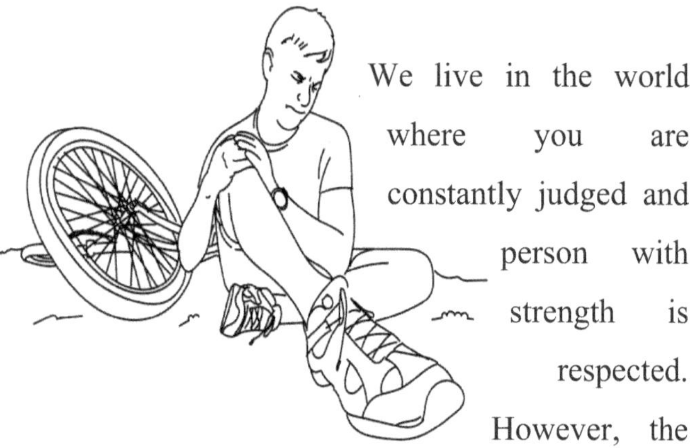

We live in the world where you are constantly judged and person with strength is respected. However, the strength is considered with physical strength or power they have. But we forget about the true strength of a person. If you want to know the true strength of a person then never focus on the money in the pocket or a muscling body.

It is here you have to measure the pain a person has endured in his/her life and still they have the strength to smile looking at you saying I am fine. They have learned to muster up the power from within to spread positive vibes around the world.

It is this inner strength that helps you go after your dreams without giving up. And you keep on going towards it without getting tired.

Chapter 38 "Silence To Solution"

Shouting or being loud mouth is becoming a trend now a days. People try and put pressure on others through this. They use this tactic to impose themselves on person with soft nature. But sometimes silence is the path to solution. It does not mean that you have given up on your dreams or you have been bullied by the loud mouths. Nor does it mean that you have compromised with your standards.

It is just that the time is not right for you to speak. Be silent and build yourself up because you need all the strength that you can muster to have what you aimed for. Time will be right when you will speak but not by words by your deeds.

In this process you have used the power of silence to find the solution of things that otherwise may have been difficult to handle. Again, with silence as your guide you tend to take better decisions and quality of your life improves.

Chapter 39 "Asking For Help Is Not Weakness"

The world we live in has numerous pre-defined notions to not allow you to feel vulnerable. The patriarchy in society talks a lot about masculinity. And this means you are tough guy who does not feel pain. To be clear you should not feel pain.

Asking for help is also looked as sign of weakness. You are not supposed to ask for help but built self alone. People forget that you do not have solution to all the problems. And knowing this helps you lessen the burden on self. Also, when you accept this reality, you move one step to finding solution.

Not asking for help and thinking I can do everything, keeps on fuelling the Ego. And when Ego becomes bigger than what it should be then it will damage your life. Just think of a person filled with Ego working in the office is not open to listening to his fellow workers, hampering the growth of the organization.

Similarly, at home the person who takes most of the decision for the family has Ego, he will not listen to the suggestions by his kids or wife. He feels offended when they don't listen to his wrong decision. This over a period of time hampers the bonding in the family and all the members suffer.

However, when you are open to seek help from others without letting your ego in between. You open yourself to less suffering and more growth. This growth is at personal and professional level. You are not weak but an open person who enjoys happiness and support from others around him.

Chapter 40 "Harshest Of The Environment Produce Most Beautiful Creations"

Mother nature is a wonderful teacher. Teaching us life lessons with real live examples to see. There are people who cry in simplest of challenges. As they feel weak or think themselves as the victim of circumstances. They fail to gather enough strength which causes suffering in their life.

Let us look into the nature as the harshest of environment have some of the most beautiful and useful creations. They have unique abilities helping them to survive these difficult environments. They are admired for their amazing adaptability towards these difficult conditions.

Similarly, people who go through tough times in their life from their early stage are role models of never giving up and enduring life. They learn at an early stage of their life that life is not to sit and cry on what you have lost or what was missed.

In fact, it is to keep upgrading self to fulfil your life's purpose. If you are open to learning, you will learn from your tough times and make the right changes into bettering self. As you find the purpose of your life.

Being open and mindful helps you to gain strength and keep facing life's challenges.

Chapter 41 "Wounds Heal When We Accept"

Our life journey helps us to learn and grow as an individual. This growth is more related to the spiritual and mental levels. It is because you learn to start handling the situations better with less fuss and confusion in your head. This ultimately brings greater clarity needed for a peaceful life.

Let us just consider the people with the prettiest of smile. Most often or not they have deepest of wounds. But they have learned the important lesson of life that is to accept and heal. They have learned the art and science of life.

This art is to remain clear headed even during life's toughest challenges. It does not mean they do not feel other emotions that every other person experiences.

They know when to let those tears do their job and when to stay strong as rock that even toughest of situation cannot perturb them.

They know world is filled with scavengers but they also know world has angels. Let me put a little more clarity in it by an example. There people whom you will encounter in your life who are similar to scavengers. This means these people wait for you to get tired or worn out then attack you.

In other way they are so self-filled that they do not bother about anyone else. At offices you will see this special class of people who take credits of your work and in community they can be family, relatives or so-called friends who will not want you to try but themselves will do it. This, is their special way to outclass you.

This does not mean that all are like that and there are good people too. As the people who have really toughen up while learning to believe. Believe in goodness in all and give chance to show that goodness. On the other hand, it should not be considered their shortcoming. As they are warriors not the worriers. They know when to take the control, after all it is time to grow.

Do you resonate with it? If your answer is in affirmative then you should prepare a small journal where you can right on daily or weekly basis about what hurt you and how you accepted it. And remember that acceptance should not lead to self-pity but to strengthen you.

Once you know what needs to be accepted and what needs to be mended then you will never find yourself mourning about challenges in life. Also, it will help you become alert to all negative and positive signs.

Chapter 42 "The Blooming Takes To Be Patience"

Let us put your imagination to work, think of your life, it is like the bud that slowly opens its petals to bloom into a beautiful flower. When you see nature, it gives you message to be patience with self and not worry. Because you are that beautiful flower which needs the time to slowly bloom into the real beautiful you. This is the beauty of unfolding life.

The path to self-growth cannot be had by rushing things. It requires you to be at peace with self and have patience. The process at times may be slow but is progressive. This progress helps you become strong step by step. With time you learn to gain the strength and bloom to show your beauty.

Social Awareness About Rare Diseases

What Is Hemophilia?

Hemophilia is a rare congenital bleeding disorder in which the patient suffers from prolonged bleeding due to extremely low level or no production of blood clotting factor in their body. In severe hemophilia patients even suffer from spontaneous bleeds into their joints, muscles, tissues or vital body organs that may lead to disability or death if not treated on time. Most of the cases the hemophiliacs become permanent disable due to lack of treatment and rehabilitation post bleeding into their joints or muscles. The treatment is costly factor injection that is transfused intra venous to them. Two common types of Hemophilia are Hemophilia A due to lack of factor 8 and Hemophilia due to lack of factor 9.

The prevalence of hemophilia is around 1 male in every 5000 males for Hemophilia A and 1 male in every 8000 males for Hemophilia B. There are 67% cases with hereditary history in the family but staggering 33% cases are first time with no previous family history. The males are patients and females are carrier of the disease. But in severe cases even the females start to show the symptoms with bleeding and blue patches.

For treatment of Hemophilia A medicine named anti-hemophilia factor 8 or just factor 8 injection is given. For treating Hemophilia B medicine factor 9 injection is given. The dosage is dependent on the type of bleed, severity of bleed, site of bleed and the weight of the person to help raise the factor level in the body.

The most common symptoms include non-stop bleeding of the cut, spontaneous bleed from the gums, bleeding in the urine, bleeding from the nose, bleeding in the GI tract without being hurt, bleeding and swelling in the joints or muscles. You can also see black or dark blue spots or patches on the body which may pain on touching at any stage of life. These patches are very common in toddler to young age.

About The Publisher

The publisher of this book titled "The Unfolding Life" by Manoj Kumar Singh is **"Power In Me Foundation."** As the name suggest it is a Trust, that works on sustainable development model. It is established to work for the welfare of the people with rare diseases and their families. Publishing is one of the activities to help raise funds to carry out the activities aimed to creating awareness about various rare diseases, provide scholarships for studies, to provide for livelihood training, to provide for healthcare training, to establish centers for their care and various other objectives for social causes.

The authors associated with us follow the same vision to make the society a better place through their creative writing. We encourage raw talents with time-to-time guidance and exposure through our creative platform Ruh-E-Mohabbat by supporting and promoting them.

For any query on our publishing services, or supporting our cause to create awareness about rare diseases while empowering them you can reach us at mpowerinme@ gmail.com. You can even call/whatsapp at +91-8851537816.

www.ingramcontent.com/pod-product-compliance
Lightning Source LLC
Chambersburg PA
CBHW071250150726
48001CB00018B/703